NEPENTHE

A Taste of Inspiration

By:
James Nathaniel Evans

Cadmus Publishing
www.cadmuspublishing.com

Copyright © 2021 James Nathaniel Evans

Published by Cadmus Publishing
www.cadmuspublishing.com
Port Angeles, WA

www.cadmuspublishing.com

ISBN: 978-1-63751-110-7
Library of Congress Control Number: 2021921610

All rights reserved. Copyright under Berne Copyright Convention, Universal Copyright Convention, and Pan-American Copyright Convention. No part of this book may be reproduced, stored in a retrieval system, or transmitted in any form, or by any means, electronic, mechanical, photocopying, recording or otherwise, without prior permission of the author.

This is a work of fiction; therefore, names, characters, places, and incidents are the products of the author's imagination or are used fictitiously. Any resemblance to actual events, locales, or persons, living or dead, is entirely coincidental.

INTRODUCTION

NEPENTHE is anything that causes one to forget their sorrow and pain. It also was a drug that was used in the ancient times as a remedy for grief.

Unlike the ancients with their method of alleviating one's pain from the conscious. I, too, believe that my thoughts of inspiration and love have the same nexus and effectancy.

Each kind thought that you read within this book will captivate your attention both mentally and spiritually.

And it is for this reason alone I convey these poetic thoughts to my readers. Enjoy!!

INSPIRATIONAL WORDS

God allows us to experience the low points of life, in order to teach us lessons we could not learn in any other way. The way we learn these lessons is not to deny the feelings, but to find the meaning underlying them.

TABLE OF CONTENTS

INSPIRATION
1. Teach Me
2. Everything
3. The Voice from Within
4. A Dream of Many
5. Wonderful Blessings
6. Introspection
7. Poetry of Proverb
8. Optimistic
9. Fruitful Thoughts
10. Appreciation
11. Awaken
12. The Cries of America
13. Hidden Tears
14. I Miss You
15. Just Believe
16. Sweet Dreams
17. The Creator
18. Prayer of Remembrance
19. Somalia
20. Beyond Yesterday
21. Reflection
22. Silent Cry
23. Love Never Dies
24. Caught Up
25. Slow Pain
26. Worldly Ways
27. Virtues of Life
28. Reality Bites
29. Socrates Cries in Vain
30. Judge Me Not

31. Give Me Not
32. Count Your Blessings
33. Give Me A Chance
34. Fortitude
35. The Souls of Hades
36. Imagine
37. Immortal Tears

STRUGGLES
38. Poetic Blues
39. Stolen Away
40. Have We Forgotten?
41. Poverty
42. Power To The People
43. Defying The Odds
44. Who Am I?
45. Buffalo Soulja
46. Assata Speaks
47. A Breath of Fresh Air
48. No Choice
49. Black World
50. Adversaries
51. Pendulum
52. My Brother's Keeper
53. Whatever Happened
54. The Struggle Continues
55. Motherland
56. Locked Away
57. When Liberty Cries
58. Cognizance
59. I'm A Soulja
60. Unbreakable

LOVE
- 61. Sapphire
- 62. A Song of Praise
- 63. The Nature of Love
- 64. More Than Words
- 65. Black Woman
- 66. A Prisoner of Love
- 67. Promise Well Kept
- 68. Pain Is Love
- 69. Waiting On Love
- 70. Keeping It Real
- 71. A Fool for Love
- 72. The Tears I Cried
- 73. Tears of A Clown
- 74. Torn Apart
- 75. Déjà vu
- 76. Consolation
- 77. Mademoiselle
- 78. Wishful thinking
- 79. Images of You
- 80. Isis
- 81. Nzinga
- 82. That Smile of Yours
- 83. I Think of You!
- 84. Call to Your Mother
- 85. Antiquity

INSPIRATION

JAMES NATHANIEL EVANS

1.
TEACH ME

DO UNTO ME AS I DO UNTO YOU,
TEACH ME WISDOM SO I MAY GROW TOO

TEACH ME TO LOVE AND NOT TO SHOW HATE,
TEACH ME TO HELP AND NEVER TO FORSAKE

TEACH ME TO REASON AND CORRECT MY MISTAKES,
TEACH ME TO OVERLOOK WHAT OTHERS CAN'T TAKE

TEACH ME TO BUILD WHAT DOUBT CAN'T CREATE,
TEACH ME TO PONDER FOR RIGHTEOUSNESS' SAKE

TEACH ME TO RESPECT THOSE SMALL AND GREAT,
TEACH ME

2.

EVERYTHING

FOR EVERY CHILD, THERE IS A MOTHER,
FOR EVERY RACE, THERE IS A COLOR.

FOR EVERY SISTER, THERE IS A BROTHER,
FOR EVERY CHALLENGE, THERE IS A STRUGGLE.

FOR EVERY SMILE, THERE IS A FROWN,
FOR EVERY BEAT THERE IS A SOUND.

FOR EVERY RIGHT, THERE IS A WRONG,
FOR EVERY THRONE, THERE IS A CROWN.

FOR EVERY PROMISE, THERE IS A DREAM,
FOR EVERY KING, THERE IS A QUEEN.

FOR EVERY WOMAN, THERE IS A MAN,
FOR EVERY ROAD, THERE IS A END

EVERYTHING IS EVERYTHING

3.
THE VOICE FROM WITHIN

INSPIRATION SPEAKS ELOQUENTLY,
DURING MOMENTS OF HARDTIMES.
PLACING ONE ABOVE ADVERSITY,
AND THE DOUBTS WITHIN THEIR MINDS.

HER WORDS OF WISDOM ARE DELIGHTFUL,
AND CAPTIVATING IN EVERY WAY.
THEY ARE THE EPITOME OF VITAMINS,
WHICH ONE NEEDS FROM DAY TO DAY.

SHE'S THE SOURCE OF EDENIC BEAUTY,
THAT GROWS NOT ON EARTHLY GROUND.
THOUGH MANY SEARCH HER CARNALLY,
SHE HAS YET TO BE FOUND.

LIKE THE COMFORT OF A GOOD WOMAN,
AND THE LOVE FROM ONE FAITHFUL FRIEND.
THUS, IS THE POWER OF INSPIRATION,
THAT CAN ONLY BE HEARD FROM WITHIN.

4.

A DREAM OF MANY

I HEARD THE WISDOM OF SOLOMON,
QUOTED THE BOOK OF PSALMS.
FOUGHT THE BATTLE OF DAVID,
AND WATCHED THE DEATH OF JOHN.

BROKE THE CHAINS OF SAMSON,
SUFFERED THE PAIN OF JOB.
ESCAPED THE HANDS OF PHAROAH,
WHILE DISCOVERING THE ANCIENT SCROLLS.

WALKED IN THE SANDALS OF MOSES,
SEEN THE BEAUTY OF SHEBA.
CROSSED THE DESERT OF ARABIA,
AND WASHED THE FEET OF JESUS.

SPOKE WITH THE ANGEL GABRIEL,
THEN READ THE HOLY QURAN.
MADE PRAYER WITH THE PROPHET,
JUST BEFORE DAWN

WITNESSED THE FAITH OF DANIEL,
FELT THE BETRAYAL OF CHRIST.
HEARD THE DENIAL OF PETER,

WHEN OTHERS THREATENED HIS LIFE.

TASTED THE FORBIDDEN FRUIT,
AND WATCHED THE FALL OF MAN.
WHILE WAKING FROM MY SLUMBER,
WITH THE BOOK OF GOD IN MY HAND

5.
WONDERFUL BLESSINGS

IN THE EARLY MORNING HOURS,
WHEN I LOOK TO THE HEAVENS.

I GIVE PRAISE TO THE CREATOR,
FOR ALL MY BLESSINGS.

WHO BLESSED ME WITH INSIGHT,
SO I COULD PERCEIVE CREATION.

AND THOSE WHO ARE INCOMPETANT,
I CAN TEACH THEM WITH PATIENCE.

WHO BLESSED ME WITH KNOWLEDGE,
SO I COULD BELIEVE IN THE UNSEEN.

WHILE MATERIALIZING MY GOALS,
BETTER KNOWN AS DREAMS.

WHO BLESSED ME WITH SYMPATHY,
SO I COULD FORGIVE OTHERS.

WHO MAY HAVE BEEN MY ENEMY,
BUT NOW THEY ARE MY BROTHER.

WHO BLESSED ME WITH COURAGE,
SO I COULD SPEAK OUT AND FIGHT.

BY ASSISTING THE POOR,
WHO'VE BEEN DEPRIVED OF THEIR RIGHTS.

WHO HAS BLESSED ME WITH EMOTIONS,
SO I MAY EXPERIENCE LOVE.

WHILE SHOWING MY COMPASSION,
TO A COLD-HEARTED WORLD.

WHO BLESSED ME WITH TRUTH,
SO I MAY NOT FOLLOW LIES.

AND BY UNDERSTANDING THIS,
I HAVE INDEED BECOME WISE.

SO BY HIS LOVELY GRACE,
I SLOWLY EMPLOY MY PEN.

THANKING GOD FOR THESE BLESSINGS,
WITH THE WORDS OF AMEN.

6.
INTROSPECTION

I'VE LEARNED TO LOVE MY ESSENCE,
WHICH REFLECTS MY CHARACTER AND DEEDS.

I'VE LEARNED TO STAY POSITIVE,
WHEN OTHERS WOULD DISAGREE.

I'VE LEARNED TO HARNESS MY POTENTIALS,
DESPITE THE SHADES OF TIME.

I'VE LEARNED TO UTILIZE MY KNOWLEDGE,
BY EDUCATING MY MIND.

I'VE LEARNED TO GROW IN WISDOM,
WHEN OTHERS REFUSE TO CHANGE.

I'VE LEARNED TO BE AN EXAMPLE,
BY DOING RIGHTEOUS THINGS.

I'VE LEARNED!!

7.
POETRY OF PROVERB

I YEARN FOR KNOWLEDGE, WISDOM AND UNDERSTANDING FOR THEY ARE SUPERB.

SO I CONSULTED WITH KING SOLOMON IN THE BOOK OF PROVERBS.

HE WAS VERY KNOWLEDGABLE AND ENLIGHTENING ON EVERY QUESTION.

WHICH MADE ME APPRECIATE HIS WISDDOM AND HIS VIRTUOUS MESSAGE.

IN CHAPTER EIGHTEEN VERSE TWENTYFOUR HE SHOWED ME A REAL FRIEND,

THAT COMPELS ME TO BE APPRECIATIVE AND LOOK MORE FORM WITHIN

HE LEAD ME THROUGH THE BOOK OF PROVERBS EVERY STEP WITH EASE,

THEN ADVISED ME WISELY TO NEVER PLACE BAD HABITS OVER MY NEEDS.

IT'S BETTER TO BE PATIENT THAN PROUD HE SAID,

ONE GETS WHAT HE WANTS, THE OTHERS HAVE IT TAKEN AWAY INSTEAD.

THOSE WORDS ILLUMINATED MY PATH AND CHANGED MY OWN PERSONAL VIEWS,

AND HELPED ME TO UNDERSTAND THE THINGS I ONCE NEGLECTED AND MISUSE.

SO IT'S NOT HARD TO SEE OR EVEN UNDERSTAND,

WHY GOD WOULD MAKE KING SOLOMON THE WORLD'S MOST WISEST MAN.

I SHARE WITH YOU HIS ADAGES OR SHALL SAY HIS POSITIVE WORDS.

I MUST LOVE YOU, OR WHY ELSE WOULD I GIVE YOU THIS POETRY PROVERB?

8.
OPTIMISTIC

Black, bold and beautiful,
have embellished my life and views.

To love, support and understand,
the path I now pursue.

Struggled have I not,
from the shadows of pain and loss.

Where burdens become conspicuous,
and hearts bleed from remorse.

How can one drown sorrow?
When it poisons the very soul.

The essence that maketh men,
to live, learn and grow.

Even though I'm optimistic,
I'm still confronted by fear.

That burns inside my subconscious,
like a flaming African spear.

Temptation speaks deceptively,
as my faith leans toward God.

Challenging my integrity
and everything I stand for.

With patience I stay focused,
Keeping my mind strong and free.

A sign of my ambition,
that reflects the real me…

9.
Fruitful Thoughts

Cast thy bread upon the water,
And it shall return in many days.

Bless thou child with knowledge,
and it shall improve his ways.

Let peace be thou gladness,
as truth relieves thy heart.

Teach by good example,
but first secure one's thought.

Listen only to the wise,
who express positive views.

By believing this truth,
you can become wise too.

Let not trouble fret thee,
nor move thy hands to war.

Fight only in one's defense,
and protect that which is yours.

Knowledge begat wisdom,
for they are one and the same.

Learn to utilize their means,
To avoid a life of pain.

10.
APPRECIATION

I've made many promises,
But only broke a few.

And those I did fulfill,
I credit them to you.

I credit you for your support,
through my ups and downs.

By encouraging me to smile,
When I usually would frown.

I credit you for your love,
when I was full of hate.

Your taught me to reason,
by not showing haste.

I credit you for your time,
when I didn't have a friend.

You told me not to worry,
and let God step in.

So that's why I'm promising,
to remain faithful and true.

By showing my appreciation,
with a simple, Thank you.

11.

AWAKEN

God, do wake me when I'm asleep,
So I may learn to be wise.
Show me your wisdom and truth,
Each day that I strive.

Strengthen me when I'm weak,
When no one seems to care.
Show me your wisdom and truth,
So I may overcome my fears.

Enlighten me when I struggle,
So others may believe.
Show me your wisdom and truth,
In that reality be conceived.

Do protect me when I'm lost,
When no light seems to shine.
Show me your wisdom and truth,
As I journey through time.

Do wake me when I'm asleep,
So I may understand you more.
Show me your wisdom and truth,
Which I failed to see before.

12.
THE CRIES OF AMERICA

WHO HEARD THE CRIES OF AMERICA?
AND FELT HER MOST MEMORABLE PAIN.

WHEN THE WORLD TRADE CENTER WAS DEMOLISHED,
BY THE USE OF AIRPLANES.

WHO SEEN THE UNFORGETTABLE MOMENT?
WHEN THOUSANDS OF PEOPLE LOST THEIR LIVES.

WHILE WE WATCH FROM OUR T.V. SCREENS,
WITH TEARS IN OUR EYES.

WHO FELT THE NEED FOR REVENGE?
WHEN DESTRUCTION MADE HER DISPLAY.

BY TAKING THE LIVES OF INNOCENT MEN,
IN THE MOST HORRENDOUS WAY.

WHO SEEN THE UNITY OF THE PEOPLE?
WHO STOOD IN THE NAME OF GOD.

URGING FOR RETALIATION,
AGAINST THOSE WHO PROMOTED WAR.

WHO SEEN THE TORCH OF AMERICA?
WHEN ITS FLAMES PIERCED THE NIGHT.

RESTORING PEACE TO THE PEOPLE,
WHO NO LONGER HAD TO LIVE IN FRIGHT.

13.

HIDDEN TEARS

BEYOND THESE WALLS OF SOLITUDE,
MY DREAMS LIVE AS YESTERDAY.

AND I'M CONTENT TO BUILD FOR TOMORROW,
KNOWING MY FAITH HAS NOT FADED AWAY.

I WITNESS THE DEMISE OF CLOSE FRIENDS,
AND MY HEART WEAKENS INSIDE.

I TRY TO UNDERSTAND THESE CHANGES,
BUT MOST OF ALL SYMPATHIZE.

PAST MEMORIES OF ABANDONMENT,
OFTEN PLAY IN MY MIND.

CREATING THOUGHTS OF RESENTMENT,
WHICH I CAN NO LONGER HIDE.

NO WORDS COULD EVER DEFINE,
THIS EMPTINESS THAT I HOLD.

IT WOULD BE LIKE TRYING TO FIND HEAVEN,
BEYOND THE REALM OF A LOST SOUL.

BUT THEN THE THOUGHT OF A NEW DAY,
APPEARS BEFORE MY VERY EYES.

CAUSING ME TO ALLEVIATE THE PAIN,
THAT WAS ONCE BURIED DEEP INSIDE.

14.

I MISS YOU

I MISS YOUR EVERY THOUGHT,
I MISS YOUR EVERY HUG.

I MISS YOUR EVERY GOOD MORNING,
WHICH YOU EXPRESSED WITH SO MUCH LOVE.

I MISS YOUR EVERY LAUGH,
I MISS YOUR EVERY SMILE.

I MISS YOUR EVERY THANK YOU,
WHICH YOU TOLD ME AS A CHILD.

I MISS YOUR EVERY SONG,
I MISS YOUR EVERY CRY.

I MISS YOUR EVERY TEAR,
WHEN YOU SAID TO US "GOODBYE".

I MISS YOU!!

15.
JUST BELIEVE

DREAMS ARE MADE TO BECOME TRUE,
UNTO THOSE WHO BELIEVE.

BECAUSE THERE IS NOTHING IN THIS WORLD,
THAT WE CAN'T FAITHFULLY ACHIEVE.

IF YOU HAVE GOALS AND DREAMS,
NEVER LET THEM DIE.

KEEP YOUR TRUST IN GOD,
AND HE WILL SURELY PROVIDE.

YES!! SOMETIMES WE HAVE DOUBT,
AND OUR FAITH BECOMES WEAK.

BUT WE CAN NEVER GIVE UP,
UNTIL WE TRULY SUCCEED.

SO CONTINUE TO BELIEVE,
IN HOPE THAT YOUR DREAM COMES TRUE.

KNOWING THAT ALL ACHIEVEMENTS,
FIRST BEGIN WITH YOU.

16.
SWEET DREAMS

Real dreams are said to come true,
unto those who believe in God.

Never compromising their faith,
no matter how bad the odds.

Time seems to pass for eternity,
as hearts become suddenly cold.

Defying the power of their mind,
which can help them achieve their goals.

Nothing is certain in this life,
and we should understand this truth.

Knowing dreams will only materialize,
based on the things we are willing to do.

It's only then we breathe freely,
and embrace the power of prayer.

Which God will answer gracefully,
unto all who are real and sincere.

17.

THE CREATOR

He's the light to the heaven and stars,
He's the thunder behind the floating clouds.

He's the voice that we hear in our thoughts,
He's the love that we feel within our hearts.

He's the mountains that stand firm and tall,
He's the spirit that lives in us all.

He's the word that has manifested true,
He's God who created both me and you.

18.
PRAYER OF REMEBERANCE

LORD, YOU KNOW THAT YOU ARE THE ONE WHO CREATED ME,
AND YOU HELPED ME TO SEE THINGS I COULDN'T SEE.

LORD, YOU GAVE ME HOPE WHEN THERE WAS NONE TO GIVE,
AND YOU SHOWED ME A BETTER WAY TO RIGHTEOUSLY LIVE.

THIS IS WHY I'M SEEKING YOUR SPIRITUAL TRUTH,
BECAUSE I NOW UNDERSTAND THE THINGS I'VE BEEN THROUGH.

ONE WHO HAS BEEN MISLED BY THE STREETS INDEED,
NOT TO MENTION LOSING MY FATHER AT THE AGE OF THREE

NOW LORD, YOU KNOW THAT WILL AFFECT ANYBODY,
BEING RAISED UP WITH A BURDEN NEVER DEPARTING.

THIS EMPTINESS DROVE ME TO A LIFE OF CRIME,
BY SELLLING DRUGS TO MY OWN RACE AND KIND.

I KNOW IT'S WRONG TO SELL DRUGS PERIOD,
BUT I WAS HARDHEADED AND JUST WOULDN'T LISTEN.

I ASKED MYSELF WHY DIDN'T MY FAMILY KNOW,
I GUESS THEY DID BECAUSE THEY SUFFERED ALSO.

SO PLEASE LORD, TAKE AWAY MY PAIN AND STRIFE,
AND RECTIFY MY PROBLEMS BY CHANGING MY LIFE.

THIS IS ALL I REQUEST AT THIS HOUR OF PRAYER,
PROTECT ME LORD AND SHOW ME YOU CARE.

19.

SOMALIA

FROM THE SHADOW OF DARKNESS,
I EMERGED AS A KING.
READY TO CONQUER ANY OBSTACLE,
LIKE THE "LORD OF THE RING".

MY TEARS TURN TO MOTIVATION,
AND MY FAITH GROWS STRONGER.
PUTTING AWAY THE EVIL VICES,
WHILE THE IGNORANT STILL PONDER.

MY BLESSINGS DESCEND LIKE RAIN,
WITH NEW HOPE AND VISION.
HELPING MY MIND TO GRAVITATE,
TOWARD MAKING BETTER DECISIONS.

THE HOLY BOOK IS MY AMMUNITION,
AND THE KEY TO MY SUCCESS.
SOMETHING EVERY SOULJAH MUST HAVE,
OR SHALL I SAY POSSESS?

INTEGRITY, I HAVE NOT COMPROMISED,
NOR BARTER FOR A MEASLY PRICE.
IT'S THE VIRTUE I'M WILLING TO DIE FOR,
AND A PRINCIPAL OF A SOULJAH LIFE.

SO DARK SHADOWS DON'T ALLUDE ME,
NOR IMPEDE THE LIGHT OF TRUTH.
KNOWING THEY ARE ONLY SMALL REMINDERS,
OF THE THINGS I ONCE PURSUED.

20.
BEYOND YESTERDAY

Beyond the streams of yesterday,
old memories breathe new life and pride.

Taking away the soul's discomfort,
which silently rages inside.

Though hope pierces the shallow grounds,
the seed of light refuses to show.

Erupting an emotion storm,
that only faith could withhold.

Yes!! Life has shown many wonders,
And the beauty of nature's kiss.

A feeling so unexplainable,
but yet seems to exist.

Beyond the streams of yesterday,
I dream wearily of tomorrow.

Yearning to embrace tranquility,
From a prison of pain and sorrow.

21.
REFLECTION

The last time I seen my father,
he was headed for the door.

Speaking words of vulgarity,
which he never spoke before.

I couldn't understand it all,
because I was only a kid.

But I always seem to wonder,
of what my father really did.

Momma somehow stayed strong,
With the problems we were facing.

She taught me to be positive,
But most of all have patience.

I believed in her words,
Knowing she appeased my pain.

A feeling of joy,
That I can hardly explain.

Though I hold no strife,
For what my father done.

I just want him to realize,
I'm still his son.

22.
SILENT CRY

SHALL I FLEE FROM MY DEMONS,
WHEN THEY ONLY EXIST AS I?

CREATED WITH A PURPOSE,
BUT YET HIDDEN FROM THE EYES.

THEY SPEAK IN A LANGUAGE,
NOT FOREIGN TO THE SOUL.

THAT COMPEL THE EMOTIONS TO SIMMER,
AND THE MIND TO LOSE CONTROL.

THEY LAUGH IN THE SHADOWS,
WHICH I CANNOT SEE.

JUST TO MOCK AT MY FAILURE,
AND TO BRING ME MISERY.

LIES ARE THE TOOLS,
THEY USE AND POSSESS.

WHICH DEPRIVE THE HEART OF PEACE,
AND ANY MEANS OF SUCCESS.

TO OVERCOME MY DEMONS,
I HAVE LEARNED TO INVEST.

BY SPENDING MY TIME WISELY,
AND FOLLOWING WHAT'S BEST.

23.
LOVE NEVER DIES

THERE ARE SOME THINGS IN LIFE,
THAT WE CANNOT DENY.

LIKE THE PAIN WE FEEL,
WHEN OUR LOVED ONES DIE.

SO MANY MEMORIES,
OFTEN MAKE US CRY.

A SIGN OF LOVE,
THAT WE HOLD DEEP INSIDE.

THEIR PRESENCE, THEIR LAUGHS,
AND THEIR CAPTIVATING CHARM.

WILL FOREVER RESIDE,
WITHIN OUR RESTLESS ARMS.

GIVING US THE STRENGTH,
TO STAND AND PRAY.

DESPITE THE LONELINESS,
WE EXPERIENCE ALONG THE WAY.

BUT THE MOMENT WILL COME,
THAT WE SHALL EMBRACE AGAIN.

AS WE UNFOLD OUR LOVE,
FOR THE LOSS OF FAMILY AND FRIENDS.

24.

CAUGHT UP

Captivated by life's foolish games,
an innocent soul dwindling in pain.

Built up rage trying to change,
how much more should I wage?

Striving to find a better way,
to relieve the hurt I feel each day.

Resentment of failure I carry inside,
while trying to swallow my manly pride.

All I've experienced and all I've seen,
still remain as a fading dream.

Sorrow or happiness, what shall it be,
for a struggling soul to find its peace?

25.
SLOW PAIN

RIGOR AND EXHAUST,
HOPE CRIES NEW TEARS.

OVERWHELMED BY PROMISES,
WHICH BROUGHT ONLY DESPAIR.

AS THE DAY TURNS INTO THE NIGHT,
EMOTIONS DO THE SAME.

BUT THE TREACHERY OF INNOCENCE,
WILL FOREVER REMAIN.

SOON FAITH WILL UNFOLD,
MAN'S CRIMSON PAST.

WHILE LIES BURST FORTH,
LIKE THE SHATTERING OF GLASS.

RIGOR AND EXHAUST,
HOW CAN ONE SURVIVE?

FROM A WORLD OF CALAMITY,
THAT BURNS FROM INSIDE.

RIGOR AND EXHAUST

26.
WORLDLY WAYS

Greed has no consciousness,
as a blind man has no sight.

Though man becomes prosperous,
he rarely finds true light.

The soul has no shadows,
as a coward has no heart.

Though man falls in love,
his mind remains in doubt.

Diamonds have no impurity,
as time has no end.

Though man strives for perfection,
he still commits sins.

Jealousy has no wages,
as hell has no depth.

Though man builds his fortune,
he keeps nothing for himself.

Vanity has no reverence,
as idols have no life.

Though man resents salvation,
his soul continues to die.

27.
VIRTUE OF LIFE

GIVE ME FREEDOM, 'CAUSE SHE BELONGS TO US ALL,
WHO SITS ON THE MOUNTAIN LIKE A WINTRY FOG.

GIVE ME JUSTICE, 'CAUSE SHE IS NEVER UNJUST,
WHO SPEAKS FOR THE PEOPLE, SAYING IN GOD WE TRUST.

GIVE ME EQUALITY, 'CAUSE SHE DISPOSES OF GREED,
WHO ACCOMMODATES THE POOR WITH NEIGHBORLY NEEDS.

GIVE ME PEACE, 'CAUSE SHE OPPOSES WAR,
WHO DISMANTLES CONFLICTS, AND NOTHING MORE.

GIVE ME TRUTH 'CAUSE SHE STANDS ALONE,
LIKE A DOUBLE-EDGED SWORD, SHE'S HARD TO HOLD.

GIVE ME HOPE, 'CAUSE SHE KEEPS FAITH ALIVE,
WHO MOTIVATES THE PEOPLE, TO ALWAYS STRIVE.

28.

REALITY BITES

Seeing is truly believing,
I heard (someone) once said.

But believing in what we can't see,
Seems to be what we most dread.

Like the belief of life after death,
has anyone returned to tell?

And does anyone really know,
if there is a heaven or hell?

Has anyone ever seen God,
With the spiritual eyes I suppose?

Or do we have to wait til we die,
When both of our eyes are closed?

Some say Moses has seen God,
And I believe this too.

But it don't negate my point,
How about you?

If seeing is believing,
How long will our faith last?

In a world of mere illusions,
That shatter like broken glass.

29.
SOCRATES CRIES IN VAIN

FROM CAPTIVITY I SPEAK,
BUT MY WISDOM IS NOT HEARD.

I'M CONSIDERED A NOBODY,
DUE TO THE GOD I SERVE.

CHASTISED BY ADVERSARIES,
WHO I MISTAKE AS FRIENDS.

WHO WOULD RATHER CRUCIFY MY IMAGE,
THAN TO SEE ME ASCEND.

NO MORE REMORSE OR REGRETS,
FOR THE THINGS THEY DO.

WHO PREFER TO CAUSE BLOODSHED,
BY AVOIDING THE TRUTH.

MORAL TEARS I DO CRY,
IN THAT MY MESSAGE SUCCEED.

WHERE LIES NO LONGER EXIST,
BUT RATHER THE VIRTUES WE BELIEVE.

30.

JUDGE ME NOT

Look deep into my soul,
and tell me what you see.

It's not the color of my skin,
but the things I believe.

Judge not my color,
cause it will never change.

But rather my character,
and positive views of things.

Please don't despise me,
without knowing my name.

When in actuality,
this should bring you shame.

Black, red and white,
we are different indeed.

But it's the heart of a person,
We should try to perceive.

31.
GIVE ME NOT

Give me not jealousy,
nor malice or strife.

But give me knowledge,
to improve my life.

Give me not fortune,
nor silver or gold.

But give me wisdom,
as those of old.

Give me not praise,
nor honor or fame.

But give me understanding,
To deal with change.

Give me not lies,
nor envy or hate.

But give me respect,
so we can relate,

Give me not depression,
nor liquor or beer.

But give me confidence,
to overcome my fears.

Give me not hatred,
nor bruises or deceit.

But give me empathy,
so I may learn peace.

32.
COUNT YOUR BLESSINGS

WHEN I CLOSE MY EYES AT NIGHT,
I SAY A SHORT PRAYER TO GOD.
ASKING HIM TO STRENGTHEN MY FAITH,
SO I MAY OVERCOME THE ODDS.

IN THE DARKNESS MY HEART CRINGES,
FOR THE PAST DEEDS I'VE DONE.
ASKING GOD TO FORGIVE ME SINCERELY,
CAUSE I KNOW I WAS WRONG.

THE PRAYER IF RIGHTEOUSNESS IS HEARD,
THIS I HAVE READ MANY TIMES.
BUT WHEN I LOOK FOR FREEDOM,
I REALIZE I AM STILL CONFINED.

HAS MY FAITH WEAKENED?
THIS I ASK, TO NO AVAIL.
KNOWING A CHANGE MUST COME,
EACH DAY THAT I AM ABLE TO EXHALE.

BUT IN A MOMENT OF DESPAIR,
GOD REVEALED HIS PRECIOUS TRUTH.
BY SENDING ME A FRIEND OF COMFORT,
TO HELP ME GET THROUGH.

ONLY THEN MY HEART RECLINES,
KNOWING MY BURDENS HAVE BEEN LIFT.
AND THE MERCY I TOOK FOR GRANTED,
TURNS OUT TO BE ONE OF THE GREATEST GIFTS.

33.

GIVE ME A CHANCE

GIVE ME THE MEANS OF KNOWLEDGE,
AND I'LL TEACH BOTH THE YOUNG AND OLD.
BY SUPPLYING THEM WITH PRINCIPALS,
JUST TO HELP THEM LIVE AND GROW.

GIVE ME THE MEANS OF RELIGION,
AND I'LL CHANGE THE ILLS IN SOCIETY,
BY ERADICATING THE INJUSTICE,
AND REPLACING IT WITH EQUALITY.

GIVE ME THE MEANS OF INTEGRITY,
AND I'LL STAND FOR WHAT'S RIGHT.
BY BUILDING A STRONGER NATION.
WITH THE TOOLS OF LIFE.

GIVE ME THE MEANS OF FORGIVENESS,
AND I'LL SET THE CAPTIVE FREE,
BY SHOWING THEM A RIGHTEOUS WAY,
LIKE GOD HAS SHOWN ME.

GIVE ME A CHANCE…

34.
FORTITUDE

DESPITE MY HOPE BEING OVERSHADOWED BY MY DOUBTS,
I STILL STAND BOLD AND STRONG.

DESPITE CAPTIVITY IMPEDING MY FREEDOM,
I STILL HAVE A PLACE I CALL HOME.

DESPITE THE YEARS OF RIGOROUS STRUGGLE,
I STILL HAVE MY MIND AND HEALTH.

DESPITE THOSE WHO HATE MY COLOR,
I STILL BELIEVE IN MYSELF.

DESPITE THE SETBACKS AND SILENT CRIES,
I STILL RISE UP AND PRAY.

DESPITE THE ENDLESS TRIALS AND MISFORTUNES,
I STILL FIND THE STRENGTH FOR ANOTHER DAY.

DESPITE IT ALL, I'M STILL ME.

35.
THE SOUL OF HADES

LET NOT MY DARKNESS BE MANY,
OR MY LIGHT BE SHORT.

PRESERVE MY SOUL LORD,
FOR WITHOUT YOU I AM NAUGHT.

LET NOT INIQUITY CONSUME ME,
WITH HER CRIMSON HANDS.

WHICH HAVE ALLURED MANY SOULS,
BOTH WOMAN AND MAN.

LET NOT PASSION OVERWHELM ME,
FROM YOUR PRECIOUS TRUTH.

TEACH MY HEART TO BE ATTENTIVE,
SO I MAY STAY CLOSE TO YOU.

LET NO HADES BE MY PILLOW,
OR MY PLACE OF STAY.

GUIDE MY WEARY EYES,
SO I MAY NOT GO ASTRAY.

LET NOT HEAVEN DISSIPATE,
FROM YOUR MERCY AND GRACE.

PRESERVE MY SOUL LORD,
AND ALL THOSE WHO HAVE FAITH.

36.
IMAGINE

IMAGINE JESUS WAS BLACK,
WITH KINKY HAIR AND NEGROID FEATURES.

I WONDER HOW MANY PEOPLE TODAY,
WOULD STILL CONSIDER HIM A PREACHER.

IMAGINE JESUS WAS BLACK,
AND HIS MOTHER MARY TOO.

I WONDER HOW MANY PEOPLE TODAY,
WOULD HAVE A DIFFERENT POINT OF VIEW.

IMAGINE JESUS WAS BLACK,
AND PORTRAYED AS A SACRED IDOL.

I WONDER HOW MANY PEOPLE TODAY,
WOULD STILL BE READING THEIR BIBLES.

IMAGINE JESUS WAS BLACK,
THE VERY OPPOSITE OF WHAT WE SEE.

I WONDER HOW MANY PEOPLE TODAY,
WOULD CLAIM HIS DIVINITY?

IMAGINE JESUS WAS BLACK,
JUST IMAGINE!!

37.
IMMORTAL TEARS

STILL MY LOVE FLOWS ENDLESSLY,
FOR YOU MY SOUL CRIES.

NO OTHER COULD REPLACE YOU,
CROSS MY HEART AND HOPE TO DIE.

YOUR LOVE IS MY SWEET MELODY,
AND THIS I WOULD NOT LIE.

MY HEART IN ANGEL FORM,
WHICH SOARS BEYOND THE SKIES.

STILL THE PAIN I HOLD WITHIN,
EMERGES FROM MY FEARS.

THAT FORCE ME TO REMEMBER YOU,
WITH THESE IMMORTAL TEARS.

JAMES NATHANIEL EVANS

STRUGGLES

JAMES NATHANIEL EVANS

38.
POETIC BLUES

TO THE MISERY I CAUSED,
TO THE LIES I SPOKE.

TO THE HEARTS I RUIN,
TO THE VOWS I BROKE.

TO THE TIMES I MISSED,
TO THE FRIENDS I SCOLD.

TO THE LOVE I ABANDONED,
TO THE GAME I SOLD.

TO THE DREAMS I SHATTER,
TO THE SOULS I MISLED.

TO THE PAIN I EMBEDDED,
TO THE MOMENTS I DREAD.

TO THE DAYS I CURSED,
TO THE NIGHTS I STRUGGLED.

TO THE BLESSINGS I SQUANDERED,
TO THE PEOPLE I HUSTLED.

TO THE WOMEN I MISTREATED,
TO THE CHILDREN I DENIED,

TO THE LOVE I REJECTED,
TO THE TEARS I NEVER CRIED.

TO ALL THOSE OF INNOCENCE,
WHOM I HURT AND ABUSED,

I PLEA FOR YOUR FORGIVENESS,
WITH THESE POETIC BLUES.

39.

STOLEN AWAY

Painful cries and frivolous lies,
How many soldiers have already died?

Falsely accused and mentally abused,
For standing up while others refused.

Raging hate and devious eyes,
Bloody palms from homicide.

Flashing lights and brutal nights,
Itching fingers that were driven to fight.

Sad stories, no remorse,
Filling the news at any cost.

Broken laws and biased ways,
Still exist in modern days.

Shattered dreams and future goals,
Stolen away from struggling souls.

Stolen Away!!!

40.
HAVE WE FORGOTTEN?

HAVE WE FORGOTTEN OUR ROOTS,
AND THE THINGS WE STOOD FOR?
WHEN BLACKS WERE MADE SLAVES,
AND BROUGHT TO THESE WESTERN SHORES.

HAVE WE FORGOTTEN THE COLD NIGHTS,
OUR FOREMOTHERS PLEAD AND CRIED?
AS THEY WATCHED IN HORROR,
WHEN THEIR LITTLE ONES DIED.

HAVE WE FORGOTTEN CHATTEL SLAVERY,
AND ITS MOST NEFARIOUS PURPOSES?
THAT PLACED BLACKS ON DISPLAY,
LIKE CLOWNS IN A CIRCUS.

HAVE WE FORGOTTEN JOMO KENYATTA,
WHO WAS VIGILANT AND BOLD?
WHO DIDN'T SELL OUT HIS PEOPLE,
FOR THE PRICE OF GOLD.

HAVE WE FORGOTTEN NELSON MANDELA,
WHO THEY IMPRISONED 27 YEARS.
FOR A CRIME HE NEVER COMMITTED,
BUT YET STILL HE WAS REVERED.

HAVE WE FORGOTTEN QUEEN NZINGA,
AND ALL HER MOST COURAGEOUS ACTS?
WHEN SHE FOUGHT AGAINST COLONIALISM,
AND EVERY EUROPEAN ATTACK.

JAMES NATHANIEL EVANS

HAVE WE FORGOTTEN MALCOLM X,
THE SHINING BLACK PRINCE?
WHEN HE SPOKE ON THE GRASSROOTS,
AND THE POWER OF CONFIDENCE.

HAVE WE FORGOTTEN CORETTA KING,
FOR ALL HER WONDERFUL ENDEAVORS?
AS SHE FOUGHT AGAINST INEQUALITY,
ON A HUMANITARIAN LEVEL.

HAVE WE FORGOTTEN ROSA PARKS,
WHO REFUSED TO RETREAT?
WHEN SHE STOOD HER GROUND,
BY NOT GIVING UP HER SEAT.

AND HOW CAN WE FORGET DR. KING,
THE TORCHLIGHT OF THE STRUGGLE?
WHO SACRIFICED HIS OWN LIFE,
TO HELP THE NEEDS OF OTHERS.

HAVE WE FORGOTTEN?

41.

POVERTY

BEING TRAPPED IN THE CLUTCHES OF POVERTY,
IS LIKE BEING DELIVERED TO HELL.

CONSTANTLY SUFFERING AND COMPLAINING,
WITH ONLY THE LORD TO TELL.

POVERTY OVERSHADOWS LIKE BLACK DEATH,
FOR THOSE WHO ARE POOR AND WEAK.

A PLAGUE AMONG THE NATIONS,
WHO HAVE SUCCUMBED TO DEFEAT.

THOSE WHO HAVE MAJOR INFLUENCE,
PRETEND NOT TO SEE.

THEY WOULD RATHER BATHE IN THEIR GLORY,
THAN TO RECTIFY POVERTY.

THE CRIES OF THE CHILDREN ARE SILENT,
BUT THEIR PAIN IS FELT INDEED.

ESPECIALLY THOSE WHO HAVE CHILDREN,
AND UNDERSTAND THE MEANING OF NEEDS.

THE SIGHT OF FALLING RAIN IS A BLESSING,
UNTO THE PARCHED SOULS THAT REST.

WHO REALIZE THAT THEIR CURRENT STATE,
IS ONLY A HEAVENLY TEST.

42.

POWER TO THE PEOPLE

THERE IS NO POETIC JUSTICE,
BEHIND CRUEL HEARTS AND MINDS.

WHO PRACTICE ONLY DECEPTION,
BY KEEPING THE PEOPLE BLIND.

TRUTH THEY DISCARD,
AS LIES BECOME THEIR SCHEME.

MASQUERADING AS NEW IDEAS,
WHICH FAIRLY REMAIN AS DREAMS.

KNOWLEDGE IS DISPERSED WISELY,
TO THOSE OF POWER AND WEALTH.

WHO UTILIZE THEIR SELFISH MEANS,
BY CONTROLLING SOMEBODY ELSE.

SUPPRESSION BECOMES PARAMOUNT,
ONCE ORDER IS ESTABLISHED.

TAKING AWAY ONE'S LIVELYHOOD,
AND REDUCING THEM TO A SAVAGE.

NO POETIC JUSTICE,
THIS I'VE COME TO BELIEVE.

IN A WORLD OF POLITICAL ILLUSION,
BETTER KNOWN AS CONSPIRACY.

43.
DEFYING THE ODDS

WE SHALL OVERCOME,
WAS SUNG LONG TIME AGO.
WHEN BLACK PEOPLE WERE UNIFIED,
AND MANY WORE AFROS.

WHEN JUSTICE WAS DENIED,
BECAUSE THEIR SKIN WERE BLACK.
AND THE ONLY KIND OF EDUCATION,
WAS TO NEVER TALK BACK.

HANDCUFFED BY RACIAL SLURS,
THAT DIMINISH ONE'S PRIDE,
AND TO ASSERT ONE'S WILL,
WAS AN ACT OF SUICIDE.

MARTIN LUTHER HAD A DREAM,
BUT DIDN'T LIVE TO SEE IT,
ASSASSINATED BY EVIL PEOPLE,
AND WE STILL CAN'T BELIEVE IT.

MALCOLM X ALSO CAME ALONG,
WITH FIRE IN HIS EYES.
TEACHING US TO STAND UP,
WHEN JUSTICE WAS BEING DENIED.

FRED HAMPTON WAS THEN KILLED,
AND WE ALL KNOW BY WHO.
BUT DID WE SEE ANY REPORT,
ON THE NIGHTTIME NEWS?

BLACK PANTHERS WERE CALLED…
COMMUNIST,
A TERM THAT WAS DESPISED.
WHICH CAUSED MANY TO BE MURDERED,
WHILE OTHERS RAN FOR THEIR LIVES.

SO OUR STRUGGLE BECAME DILUTED,
AND OUR FOUNDATION WAS CRACK.
CAUSING SOME TO PRAISE THE WHITES,
WHILE OTHERS WERE HATING BLACKS.

FARRAKHAN SUDDENLY EMERGED,
LIKE A CANDLE IN THE DARK.
ASKING THE PEOPLE FOR ATONEMENT,
WITH HIS "MILLION MAN MARCH".

UNITY IS THE KEY, HE SAID,
WILL BUILD ANY NATION OR RACE.
AND ONCE WE LEARN THIS TRUTH,
THERE'S NOTHING WE CANNOT FACE.

DEFYING THE ODDS!!

44.
WHO AM I?

WITH A POSITIVE STATE OF MIND,
I SIT CONFINED WITHIN MY CHAINS.

THINKING OF A MASTER PLAN,
TO RECEIVE MY FREEDOM AGAIN.

KNOWLEDGE OF DIFFERENT KINDS,
CAN BE FOUND WITHIN MY REACH.

AS I SEARCH FOR NEW EVIDENCE,
TO REVERSE MY PAST DEFEAT.

VOICES OF THOSE WHO HAVE FAILED,
RING CLEARLY WITHIN MY EAR.

DOUBTING MY WONDEROUS STEPS,
AS I MOVE GRADUALLY BEYOND DESPAIR.

WHO AM I? WHO AM I?
THIS I QUESTION MY HEART IN VAIN.

TRYING TO FIND A HIDDEN REMEDY,
TO RELIEVE MY SOUL OF PAIN.

PERPETUAL CHAINS I DO BARE,
FOR JUSTICE HAS NOT EYES TO SEE.

ITS STANDARD HAS BECOME CORRUPT,
AND THERE IS NO FORM OF LIBERTY.
SO MY FREEDOM REMAINS DISTANT,
AND MY HEART REMAINS CONFINED.

SEEKING FOR A BETTER WAY,
TO UNLOCK THIS WORLD OF MINE.

45.
BUFFALO SOULJA

THIS POEM IS FOR THE RASTAS.
WHO BELIEVE IN THE STRUGGLE.
FIGHTING AGAINST THE SYSTEM,
AND NOT AGAINST THEIR OWN BROTHERS.

WHO RALLY IN THE STREETS,
WHENEVER INJUSTICE IS DONE.
AND WE CAN HEAR THEIR TRIUMPH,
LIKE A OLD REDEMPTION SONG.

THEY BURN THE CHALICE,
FOR RIGHTEOUSNESS' SAKE.
A SYMBOL OF THEIR FAITH,
WHICH THE UNGODLY CANNOT BREAK.

THEY REVERE "ITAL" LIVING,
AND THE HERBS FROM THE EARTH.
SOMETHING THE FOOLISH STRIVE TO DESTROY,
BECAUSE THEY REALIZE NOT ITS WORTH.

THEY MEDITATE ON VIRTUES,
TO ENRICH THEIR HEARTS AND MINDS.
WHICH HELPS TO PROMOTE TRUTH,
WHENEVER EVIL BEGINS TO RISE.

THEY BELIEVE IN KING SOLOMON,
WHO WAS KNOWN TO BE WISE.
AND ALL THE RIGHTEOUS PEOPLE,
WHO MADE A DIFFERENCE IN OUR LIVES.

46.

ASSATA SPEAKS

Black as the coal,
Was her radiant skin.
Shining like sun rays,
That reflect from within.

A model of the struggle,
For her intensity and strength.
That transformed into unity,
Which many tried to prevent.

The love of her people,
Stood the test of her foes.
Who tried to break her spirit,
And her unrelenting soul.

Impregnated by hope,
That never surrendered to defeat.
She learned to maintain,
By overcoming adversity.

Through the darkness of hatred,
And time-raging evil.
It couldn't weaken her mind,
Or the love of her people.

Justice heard her cries,
But didn't feel her pain,
So, she was compelled to speak out,
Against the negative things.

JAMES NATHANIEL EVANS

Emerging from the shadows,
To the pedestal of truth.
Leading the way for others,
Who'd been mistreated and abused.

In the echoes of liberty,
Her voice can be felt.
Motivating is to stand up,
By believing in ourselves.

47.
A BREATH OF FRESH AIR

EACH DAY, I CONTEMPLATE MY LIFE AND FUTURE GOALS,
JUST TO REALIZE THE BLESSINGS AND BEAUTY OF MY SOUL.

AND THOSE WHOM I REVERE FOR THEIR LOVE AND DEEDS,
GRADUALLY BECOME MY SILENT WHISPER TO SUCCEED.

OF COURSE, I'M CONFRONTED BY STRUGGLES AND FEARS,
THAT CAUSE ME TO DOUBT AND EVEN SHED TEARS.

BUT SOMEHOW, I'M REJUVENATED BY MY OWN AMBITION,
WHICH ALLOWS ME TO RATIONALIZE AND MAKE BETTER DECISIONS.

WILL I SURVIVE THESE CRIMSON HANDS OF TIME?
WHERE THE SHADOWS OF UNCERTAINTY INVADE ONE'S MIND.

WILL I EVER LIVE TO EMBRACE THE LIKES OF SUCCESS?
AND ENTERTAIN VANITY OR HER COUSIN DEATH.

A BREATH OF FRESH AIR, THIS I DO HAVE WITHIN,
TO LIFT MY HEART AND SPIRIT BEYOND THE PATH OF SIN.

FOR ONLY WITH THESE MEANS MY LIFE TRULY UNFOLDS,
AS I GRAVITATE TOWARD TRUTH AND THINGS I DIDN'T KNOW.

48.
NO CHOICE

NO CHOICE I SCREAM,
IN MORE WAYS THAN ONE.

WHERE THE NEW WORLD ORDER,
HAS ALREADY BEGUN.

WHERE NO RIGHTS ARE GIVEN,
TO SPEAK OUT OR STAND.

AND RELIGION BECOMES REVISED,
FOR A UNIVERSAL PLAN.

WHERE FREEDOM IS BANISHED,
AND TRUTH IS CLONED.

UNMASKING OPPRESSION,
THAT GRADUALLY TAKES FORM.

SUPERVISION IS DISPLAYED,
AND REGULATION IS ENFORCED.

TAKING AWAY ONE'S LIVELIHOOD,
FOR THIS NEW POLITICAL COURSE.

PICTURES NO LONGER EXIST,
ONLY NUMBERS AND CODES.

TRACKING ONE'S EVERY STEP,
LIKE A STANDARDIZED PAROLE.

JUSTICE BECOMES AUTONOMOUS,
NO MORE JURY TO DECIDE.

AND ONE JUDGMENT ALONE,
COULD DETERMINE IF WE LIVE OR DIE.

LEGISLATION WILL CHANGE,
TO ACCOMMODATE THE ELITE.

WHO WILL RISE TO NEW HEIGHTS,
BY SHOWING NO SIGNS OF DEFEAT?

NO CHOICE I SCREAM,
IN VAIN I HOPE NOT.

TO WARN MY FELLOW CITIZENS,
OF THIS NEW WORLD ORDER PLOT.

49.
BLACK WORLD

CAN WE IMAGINE WHAT LIFE WOULD BE,

IF EVERYTHING WAS BLACK?

NO MORE UNEMPLOYMENT,

BECAUSE OF THE EDUCATION WE LACK.

NOW HOW MANY OF US COULD BELIEVE AND ADHERE TO THAT?

NO MORE DISCRIMINATION,

BECAUSE WE WOULDN'T SEE COLOR,

NOW HOW MANY OF US WOULD TREAT BLACK PEOPLE AS THEIR BROTHERS?

NO MORE SOCIAL DIVISION,

BECAUSE WE'LL BELIEVE IN THE SAME SYSTEM.

NOW HOW MANY OF US WOULD PRACTICE SEPARATISM?

NO MORE VERBAL ABUSE,

BECAUSE WE WOULD HAVE BETTER WORDS TO USE.

NOW HOW MANY OF US WOULD STILL BE CONFUSED?

NO MORE FALSE IDENTITY,

BECAUSE OUR HISTORY WOULD NOT BE A MYSTERY.

NOW HOW MANY OF US WOULD STILL LIVE UN-RIGHTEOUSLY?

IF THE WORLD WAS BLACK AS SOME MAY WISH,

THERE'D STILL BE A PROBLEM AMONG OUR OWN RACE.

NOW HOW MANY OF US BELIEVE THAT?

50.
ADVERSARIES

It's my dream to submerge my foes,
who have plotted and planned my defeat.

Envying my rise to cognizance,
beyond the shadows of the lame and weak.

Power becomes my stage of honor,
as I move righteously about.

Speaking for what I believe in,
while others remain in doubt.

No glory is there in the grave,
so, I fight with both integrity and pride.

Undermining my enemies' intentions,
who had wished for my demise.

51.

PENDULUM

Political agenda --- shall we surrender,
A nation of war --- with no defenders.
Bless the children ---teach them wisdom,
Give them knowledge ---on better living.
Stop the violence --- do not remain silent,
Too much injustice --- for one man's tolerance.
Temple of the ancient --- truth withheld,
Those who are blind --- will never excel.
Mystical events --- no man is certain,
Life after death --- for all who searches.

52.
MY BROTHER'S KEEPER

Smile for me my brother,
and do believe this truth.
The love you've shown to me,
I'm now giving it back to you.

You have stood by my side,
through both thick and thin.
And you exemplify realness,
by remaining a good friend.

Like when I was down and out,
with little of friends and wealth.
You told me to stay strong,
and always believe in myself.

Those words I kept close,
in a real special way.
Never knowing they would change me,
and make me better today.

I remember when you said to me,
put it all in God's hands.
And now when you think about it,
those words strengthen me as a man.

So, I can't forget your love,
and the support that you've shown.
Which is one of the reasons why,
I'm still holding on.

53.
WHATEVER HAPPENED

In a world of division,
How can there be true leaders?
Who stand for righteousness,
And fight for one's freedom.

Whatever happened to the phrase,
"We Shall Overcome"?
Is this something of the past,
That can no longer be done?

Whatever happened to the Steve Biko's,
Who stood for a cause?
By fighting against Apartheid,
When times were very hard.

Whatever happened to the Huey Newton's,
Whom America despised?
Who mislead the public,
With their false images and lies?

Whatever happened to the unity,
Which mends our broken hearts?
That helped us to stay strong,
While others fell apart.

Whatever happened to the love,
That we frequently shared?
While we overcame adversity,
Through blood, sweat and tears.

Whatever happened to the phrase,
"My word is my bond"?
Is this something of the past,
That can no longer be shown?

WHATEVER HAPPENED?

54.
THE STRUGGLE CONTINUES

BLACK POWER!! BLACK POWER!!
THESE ARE THE WORDS OF A MILITANT REDEEMER,
WHO TOOK THE WORLD BY SURPRISE
WHEN HE STOOD UP AS A LEADER.

NEVER CARING FOR HIS OWN LIFE, BUT THE WELLBEING OF OTHERS,
BY SHOWING THEM HIS TRUE LOVE,
AND THEN CALLING THEM HIS BROTHERS.
SELF-INTEREST DID NOT EXIST, BECAUSE OPPRESSION WAS SO WIDE,

AND TO THINK ABOUT ONESELF WAS AN ACT OF SUICIDE.
PENNIES FOR THE CONDEMNED, FOR THEY WERE ONE AND THE SAME.
DANCING FOR THE OPPRESSOR WHO DID NOT EVEN ACKNOWLEDGE HIS NAME.
NI**GA WAS A TITLE THAT PLAYED THROUGHOUT THE DAY,

SOME GRASPED FOR REAPPROVAL, BUT ONLY TO FADE AWAY.

BLACK POWER!! BLACK POWER!!
DON'T YOU FEEL THE INSPIRATION?
BOBBY SEAL AND HUEY NEWTON WERE ALL PLAYERS HATED.

NOT LIKE SOME PIMP, WHO EXPLOITS OUR BLACK SISTERS,
BUT MORE LIKE A RULER WHO DON'T FOLD UNDER PRESSURE.
ADVERSITY DOES BEND AGAINST THE SWORD OF RESISTANCE,
BUT IT'S THE HEART OF THE PEOPLE THAT MUST BE PERSISTENT.

THE CALL FOR LIBERATION OFTEN ECHOES LIKE A DRUM,
VIBRATING THE WORLD LIKE A GIANT KING KONG.
NO-LIMIT SOLDIERS IS WHAT THE STRUGGLE IS ABOUT,
TEACHING BY EXAMPLE AND HELPING OUR PEOPLE OUT.

BLACK POWER!! BLACK POWER!!

55.

MOTHERLAND

HOW LONG WILL SHE REMAIN DESOLATED,
AND DEPRIVED OF HER NATURAL WEALTH?
FOR LIKE A PRISONER SHE HAS BECOME,
WITHIN THE CUSTODY OF SOMEONE ELSE.

SHE WEEPS BITTERLY IN THE NIGHT,
WITH TEARS ON HER CHEEKS.
AMONG ALL HER ABUSIVE LOVERS,
SHE FINDS NO PLACE TO FLEE.

HER ADVERSARIES CONSTANTLY PLOT,
DUE TO THE WEALTH WHICH SHE HOLDS.
FOR WITH HANDS OF TREACHERY,
THEY WOULD DESTROY THE YOUND AND OLD.

IS IT OF ANY IMPORTANCE,
FOR ONE TO VISUALIZE AND SEE,
THE DESTRUCTION OF A CIVILIZATION,
WHICH BROUGHT ABOUT YOU AND ME.

56.

LOCKED AWAY

My precious little queen,
you are beautiful by far.

And when I perceive heaven,
I think of my shining star.

I know one day soon,
you'll no longer be alone.

Because I'll abandon these chains,
and to you, I'll come home.

I wish I could show you,
how much you mean to me.

It would appease my soul,
just to see you're happy.

For you're my peace of mind,
and strength in here.

Your love gives me the courage,
to overcome my fears.

And there is not a day goes by,
I don't think about your love.

Knowing you're my shining star,
But most of all, my baby girl.

57.

WHEN LIBERTY CRIES

WHEN LIBERTY CRIES VERACIOUSLY,
AND AMERICA WIPES AWAY HER TEARS.

SHE NO LONGER IMPLORES FOR JUSTICE,
OR THE THING SHE SECRETLY FEARS.

THE ROAD TO HAPPINESS AND PROSPERITY,
SITS FIRMLY BEFORE HER EYES.

RESTORING HER HEART WITH CONFIDENCE,
FROM THE PAIN SHE FEELS INSIDE.

SWEET AMERICA!! SWEET AMERICA!!
HER VOICE ECHOES BEYOND THE NIGHT.

BRING SALVATION TO THE OPPRESSED,
AND THOSE SEARCHING FOR A BETTER LIFE.

SURELY, LIBERTY CRIES NOT IN VAIN,
FOR HER HEART REMAINS STRONG AND FREE.

THE EPITOME OF LOVE AND HOPE,
UNTO ALL WHO BELIEVE IN EQUALITY.

58.

COGNIZANCE

Fight me no more, my brother,
could we at least reason first?

It takes 2 to clash,
so control your outburst.

Strike me once,
Yes! You made a mistake.

Strike me twice,
It only reflects on your hate.

Of course we are men,
so, why not think as one?

How can we progress mentally,
but yet still remain dumb?

Respect is a part of us,
and it shows our inner light.

But when ignorance becomes our friend,
it only drives us to fight.

So put away the madness my brother,
and change your evil thoughts.

Cause violence never solved anything.
it just corrupts our hearts.

59.

I'M A SOULJA

I'M A SOULJA WITH NO ARMY,
BUT I'M NOT AFRAID TO DIE.
I UTILIZE MY INTELLECT,
THAT'S THE WAY I SURVIVE.

MY ADVERSARIES ARE DIMINISHED,
AND THEIR SCHEMES ARE EXPOSED.
I LEAVE THEM BROKEN AND IN DISMAY,
WITH THE KNOWLEDGE I'VE COMPOSED.

BAPTIZED BY POLITICAL AGENDAS,
WHICH EMERGE AND TAKE FORM.
CAUSING DESTRUCTION AND DISUNITY,
LIKE A TROPICAL STORM.

BOUND BY STRENGTH AND HONOR,
I SUPERSEDE THEIR AIMS.
THOSE WOULD RATHER SEE ME CAPTIVATED,
WITHIN A CAGE OF RAGE.

MY AMMUNITION IS AMBITION,
THAT ILLUMINATES THE CLOUDIEST SKIES.
HELPING THE POOR TO BECOME STRONGER,
AND THE STRONGER TO BECOME WISE.

LIKE THE RISING OF THE SUN,
MY CONFIDENCE DOES THE SAME.
MOTIVATING MY POTENTIALS,
TO DEAL WITH THE CHANGE.

60.
UNBREAKABLE

I'M A SOULJA BEHIND ENEMY LINES,
FACING BOTH ADVERSITY AND PAIN.
DEMORALIZED FOR BEING RIGHTEOUS,
DUE TO THE KNOWLEDGE I'VE OBTAIN.

CONFLICTS BECOME INEVITABLE,
AND RATIONAL CEASES TO EXIST.
WHILE BEING LOCKED UP POLITICALLY,
FOR INDICTMENT THAT SHOULD'VE BEEN DISMISS.

BROKEN DREAMS ARE OFTEN TARNISHED,
AS REMORSEFUL TEARS SILENTLY FALL.
THE REFLECTION OF A CONSCIOUS SOULJA,
WHO CONTINUE TO STAND STRONG AND TALL.

RECALCITRANT TO THE OPPOSITION,
THAT MY APPEARANCE INFURIATES THIS OPPRESSOR.
WHO VIOLATE MY CONSTITUTIONAL RIGHTS,
THEN LABEL ME AS THE AGGRESSOR.

SOME THINK THAT IT'S THE CHAINS THAT CONFINE,
BUT I DIFFER AND SAY IT'S THE BIASED LAWS.
WHICH PROMOTE ONLY SOCIAL INJUSTICE,
THE VERY EPITOME OF A PSYCHOLOGICAL WAR.

HERE I STAND CLOTHED IN MY OWN INTEGRITY,
FIGHTING AGAINST THE POWER OF THE INSATIABLE.
WHO EMPLOY EVERY TOOL OF DISSENSION,
TO DISMANTLE THE WILL FOR THE UNBREAKABLE.

HERE I AM…..

JAMES NATHANIEL EVANS

LOVE

JAMES NATHANIEL EVANS

61.

SAPPHIRE

WHERE IS MY QUEEN?
BEAUTIFUL AND BOLD.
SWEET AS THE HONEY
AND PRECIOUS LIKE GOLD.

EYES OF DIAMONDS,
AND SKIN OF SILK.
BODY OF CARAMEL,
THAT FIRMLY BUILT.

TEETH OF IVORY,
AND HANDS OF SATIN.
HEART OF CHOCOLATE,
THAT MELTS AS PASSION.

SOUL OF BEAUTY,
AND A MIND OF STRENGTH.
WINGS OF ANGELS,
WHOM HEAVENLY SENT.

LIPS OF RUBIES,
AND BREATH OF WINE.
LEGS OF JEWELS,
THAT UNIQUELY DESIGN.

FEET OF LILLIES,
AND LOCKS OF GOLD.
ARMS OF COTTON,
THAT EMBRACE AND HOLD.

JAMES NATHANIEL EVANS

WHERE IS MY QUEEN?
SO BEAUTIFUL AND BOLD.
HAS ANYONE SEEN HER?
DOES ANYONE KNOW?

WHERE IS MY QUEEN?

62.
A SONG OF PRAISE

SHE'S MY NUBIAN QUEEN,
SHE'S MY INNER STRENGTH.
SHE'S MY RADIANT LIGHT,
WHEN I'M IN NEED OF A FRIEND.

SHE'S MY EBULLIENT SMILE,
SHE'S MY CONSCIOUS PAIN.
SHE'S MY SWEET SUNSHINE,
AFTER THE POURING RAIN.

SHE'S MY HEAVENLY PEACE,
SHE'S MY GLORIOUS STRUGGLE.
SHE'S MY DIVINE GUIDANCE,
WHEN I'M CONFRONTED BY TROUBLE.

SHE'S MY VIBRANT THOUGHTS,
SHE'S MY PRECIOUS TREASURE.
SHE'S MY AFRICAN ROOTS,
WHICH GROWS BEYOND MEASURE.

SHE'S MY CLOSEST COMPANION,
SHE'S MY FAITHFUL FRIEND.
SHE'S MY CARING SISTER,
UNTIL THE VERY END.

63.
THE NATURE OF LOVE

THE NATURE OF LOVE IS IMPECCABLE,
MORE THAN WORDS CAN SAY.

IT CAN GENERATE TRUE PASSION,
IN THE MOST BEAUTIFUL WAY.

IT'S A GIFT UNTO MANKIND,
WHO EMPLOYS FREE WILL.

BUT WHEN ABUSED AND MISUSED,
IT CAN DESTROY OR EVEN KILL.

IT'S A MYSTERY UNTO MANY,
WHO HAVE NOT EYES TO SEE.

WHOSE HEARTS REMAIN CONFINED,
DUE TO THEIR OWN MISERY.

IT'S A SEA WITH NO DEPTH,
WHERE PEARLS EMERGE AND FORM.

BRING BEAUTY TO THE SURFACE,
LIKE THIS ROMANTIC POEM.

64.
MORE THAN WORDS

A TREE HAS NO FOUNDATION,
IF IT HAS NO ROOTS.

A POEM HAS NO MEANING,
IF IT CONTAINS NO TRUTH.

A FIRE HAS NO FLAME,
IF IT HAS NO FUSE.

A SOUND HAS NO RHYTHM,
IF IT HAS NO BLUES.

A MIND HAS NO PEACE,
IF IT'S CONSTANTLY CONFUSED.

AND LIFE WOULD HAVE NO MEANING,
IF I DIDN'T HAVE YOU.

65.

BLACK WOMAN

BLACK WOMAN!! BLACK WOMAN!!

OH!! HOW I LOVE YOUR CHARM.
FOR YOU ARE THE PEACE TO MY EMPTINESS,
WHENEVER I'M ALONE.

BLACK WOMAN!! BLACK WOMAN!!
BEAUTIFUL AND STRONG.
I REVERE YOUR COURAGE,
WHEN YOU TAKE YOUR THRONE.

BLACK WOMAN!! BLACK WOMAN!!
I ADORE YOUR ESSENCE.
THE EPITOME OF GOOD LOVE,
WHOM GOD GAVE AS BLESSINGS.

BLACK WOMAN!! BLACK WOMAN!!
WHO CAN DENY YOUR CROWN,
YOU'VE BEEN A MOTHER AND SISTER,
SINCE THE BEGINNING OF TIME.

BLACK WOMAN!! BLACK WOMAN!!

66.

A PRISONER OF LOVE

Last night I dreamed of a Mystical Land.
Whereas Love was a prisoner in bond and chains.

Convicted for words he never said or spoke,
He was ordered to serve life by the principal court.

While tears of resentment ran down Love's face,
He knew he was innocent, so he called on a friend.

Now Lies couldn't testify on Love's behalf,
She wasn't a credible witness, due to her deviant past.

So he called on Truth, the best lawyer in town,
Who had made a name got himself by proving others wrong.

Now on the day of the trial Love stood before the stand,
Pleading not guilty as he raised his right hand.

Question after question he answered with no surprise,
As the jury looked on with suspicion in their eyes.

Then, all of a sudden, Truth pointed down the aisle,
Calling Patience to the stand to finally testify.

She stares in the court room and calmly spoke in pride,
Saying she's not a criminal of law, just an alibi.

Then in one appalling notion, there was a vicious outcry,
Envy began accusing Hate for being the one who lied.

Then jealousy stood buoyantly only to take Hate's side,
Saying let justice be served, Love is the guilty guy.

Judge Righteous then stood and pummeled his fist,
Pointing at Jealousy who was the cause of all this.

Then Justice came along to take Hate away,
Who began to scream in defiance, saying he'll be back one day.

Love then smiled rejoicefully, almost in disbelief,
Because he knew within his heart, he would soon be free.

67.
PROMISE WELL KEPT

AS I SIT AND DWELL ON THE EVER-LASTING PAST,
I SOMETIMES FIND MYSELF GETTING MAD.
ANXIOUSLY WAITING ON A UNIQUE OPPORTUNITY,
KNOWING A SPIRITUALLY MINDED QUEEN WILL ONE DAY BE WITH ME.
SHE WOULD BE PLEASING IN THE SIGHT OF GOD,
AND THE LOVE WE SHARE WILL NEVER BE VOID.
SHE WOULD BE LOVELY, SHE WOULD BE SWEET,
SHE WOULD BE GENTLE AND VERY PETITE.
I'M JUST SITTING HER INSIDE MY ROOM,
QUIETLY HUMMING A SPIRITUAL TUNE,
PATIENCE IS A VIRTUE VERY WELL KNOWN.
OH!! HOW MY FAITH HAS SURELY GROWN.
THE WOMAN I SEEK IS COMING MY WAY,
WITH LOVE IN HER HEART THAT IS HERE TO STAY.
AND BEING UN-LADY LIKE IS NOT HER STYLE,
CAUSE ONE DAY SOON, SHE'LL BE NURTURING MY CHILD.
SO, THANK YOU, LORD FOR I NEEDED YOUR HELP,
AND I KNOW WITHOUT A DOUBT, THIS WAS A PROMISE WELL KEPT.

68.

PAIN IS LOVE

BURNING DEEP AND LOSING SLEEP,
IS THIS THE CAUSE FOR WHICH MY EYES WEEP?
A SUDDEN ITCH BENEATH THE VEINS,
TELL ME THE MYSTERY OF MY PRESENT PAIN.
IS IT LUST OR IS IT LOVE?
WHAT IS THERE TO EXPLAIN MORE OF?
SIMPLE ATTRACTION AND ALLURING SIGNS,
HAVE CAPTIVATED MY HEART AND BLEW MY MIND.
PAIN IS LOVE, THAT'S ALL I' VE FOUND.

69.
WAITING ON LOVE

I STILL WAIT PATIENTLY FOR YOU,
TO UNFOLD YOUR SLEEPING HEART.
BUT IT SEEMS THE LONGER I WAIT,
THE FARTHER WE GROW APART.

SIMMERING QUESTIONS OF IMPATIENCE,
CONSTANTLY LINGER IN MY MIND.
AS I SEEK FOR HIDDEN ANSWERS,
WHICH ONLY THE HEART CAN FIND.

COULD FEAR POSSIBLY EXIST,
IN A WORLD I THOUGHT WAS STRONG?
WHERE TRUSTED BECOMES TARNISHED,
AND SMILES TURN TO FROWNS.

MUST I PLEAD WITH REASONS,
AND NOT FIND A HIDDEN CLUE?
TO EXEMPLIFY MY FEELINGS,
THAT I NOW CARRY FOR YOU.

MUST I HOLD ON TO PROMISES,
THAT WILL ONE DAY FATALLY DIE.
WHILE I SIT WAITING FOR LOVE,
WITH BLUE TEARS IN MY EYES.

70.

KEEPING IT REAL

THIS LOVELY AND THOUGHTFUL POEM,
I NOW COMPOSE TO YOU, MY QUEEN.
FOR AIDING ME THROUGH MY STRUGGLES,
AND HELPING ME TO BELIEVE,

YOU'VE BEEN BY MY SIDE,
THROUGH BOTH THICK AND THIN.
WHICH IS ONE OF THE REASONS WHY,
I CAN CALL YOU A REAL FRIEND,

YOU NEVER FORSAKE ME,
WHEN I WAS DOWN AND OUT.
YOU TOLD ME TO KEEP THE FAITH,
WHEN I USUALLY WOULD HAVE DOUBT.

YOUR WORDS SPOKE IN VOLUMES,
AND I CONCEAL THEM INSIDE,
WHICH MADE ME STRONGER,
AND A LITTLE MORE WISE.

SO, WITH WORDS OF APPRECIATION,
I EXPRESS MY LOVE AND CARE.
THANKING FOR YOUR SUPPORT,
AND FOR ALWAYS BEING THERE.

71.
A FOOL 4 LOVE

A FOOL FOR LOVE,
YES!! THAT'S WHAT YOU ARE.
CONSTANTLY CHASING A SHOOTING STAR.
DOWN TO EARTH SHE SHAMELESSLY FALLS,
ONLY TO DRIVE YOU UP THE WALL.
DAY AFTER DAY, IT'S THE SAME OLE THING,
BACK AND FORTH LIKE A BROKEN SWING.
PLEASURE OR PAIN, WHAT SHALL IT BE?
FOR THE LIFE OF A FOOL AND HID MISERY.
A FOOL 4 LOVE, THAT'S WHAT YOU ARE.
STUCK BY LUST OF A DEVILISH HEART.
HOW MUCH MORE SHALL YOU WAGE AND SELL?
FOR THE PRICE OF LOVE THAT BROUGHT YOU
HELL.
A FOOL 4 LOVE THAT'S WHAT YOU ARE…
A FOOL 4 LOVE.

72.
THE TEARS I CRIED

A SERIOUS AND CONFUSED MAN AT HEART,
HOPING AND PRAYING FOR A BRAND-NEW START.

ALSO TRYING NOT TO CLOUD MY BRAIN,
WITH UNWANTED THOUGHTS THAT POUR DOWN LIKE RAIN.

WHO GAVE ME THE AUTHORITY TO ALTER YOU LOVE,
OR WAS THAT A CRIMINAL ACT COVERED IN MUD.

HEAR ME OUT MU BEAUTIFUL QUEEN,
I SEEK KNOWLEDGE, WISDOM AND SPIRITUAL THINGS.

DO FORGIVE ME FOR THE TIMES I'VE LIED,
WHICH CAUSE YOU TO DOUBT AND EVEN CRY.

MY HONESTY WILL HELP SUBMERGED THE STORM,
BUT WITHOUT YOUR LOVE, THIS IS ONLY A POEM.

NEVER HAS THERE BEEN A CONFUSED HEART,
PRAYING AND WISHING FOR A BRAND-NEW START.

SO PLEASE DON'T EVER SAY TO ME GOOD-BYE,
AND FORCE ME TO REMEMBER YOU WITH THE TEARS I CRIED.

73.
TEARS OF A CLOWN

I WEAR THIS MASK TO DISGUISE MY FROWN,
KNOWING THE PAIN OFTEN KEEPS ME DOWN.
I WOULD LIKE TO CHANGE WHAT I FEEL IS WRONG.
BUT SOMEHOW MY FEARS ONLY ESCALATE THE STORM.
I WISH I COULD TURN BACK THE HANDS OF TIME,
I WOULD GIVE EVERYTHING TO MAKE HER BACK MINES.
JUST TO SHOW HER THAT MY LOVE WAS REAL,
AND WIPE AWAY THESE TEARS THAT I CAN NO LONGER CONCEAL.

74.

TORN APART

O, MY PRECIOUS HELENA!
WHY MUST THOU HINDER OUR LOVE?
AND FORCE ME TO REMEMBER YOU DIS-HEARTILY.
TRULY, MY SOUL CRIES ONLY FOR THEE
IN THE ABYSS OF MY OWN AFFECTION.

WHY DOES NOT THOU SEE'ST,
THE RESENTFUL TEARDROPS IN MY EYES
AS THEY CASCADE DOWN MY CHEEK?

O, MY PRECIOUS HELENA!
SPEAK TO ME IN WORDS OF VERACITY,
IF THOU HEART CONCEAL NOT LIES
AND REASON STILL REMAINS YOUR LIGHT AND GUIDANCE.

HOW LONG MUST I CRY IN VAIN?
OR WITNESS THE DEMISE OF MY OWN LOVE?
WHILE THE WOUNDS OF DESERTION
PROTRUDE MY WILL TO LIVE ANOTHER DAY.

O, MY PRECIOUS HELENA!
TAKE AWAY THESE IMMORAL SHACKLES,
FOR TRUE LOVE CAN NEVER DIE.
NOR CAN ONE WHO IS VOID OF AFFECTION
FEEL AND KNOW REALITY WITHOUT A HEART.

O, MY PRECIOUS HELENA!
LOOK THROUGH THE WINDOW OF MY SOUL
AND TELL ME WHAT DO THOU SEE'ST?
TELL ME IN WORDS OF VERACITY
IF THOU HEART CONCEAL NOT LIES.
TELL ME!!

75.

DÉJÀ VU

OUR FORTUITOUS ENCOUNTER,
MUST BE DÉJÀ VU.
BECAUSE I'VE NEVER KNOWN LOVE,
UNTIL I MET YOU.

SOMETHING SO STRANGE,
BUT YET SO TRUE.
WHICH CAN CHANGE ONE MIND,
AND THE THINGS THEY DO.

EVER SINCE YOU ENTERED,
INTO MY LONELY LIFE.
THERE SO MUCH HAS CHANGED,
WHICH YOU MADE RIGHT.

YOUR PRESENCE ALONE,
HAS SOOTHED MY STORM.
BY ALLEVIATING THE PAINS,
WHICH EMOTIONALLY BURN.

THAT'S WHY I EXPRESS,
THESE WORDS OF TRUTH,
FOR THIS WONDERFUL ENCOUNTER
WITH DÉJÀ VU.

76.
CONSOLATION

YOU HAVE BEEN MY CONSOLATION,
SINCE FREEDOM HAS ELUDED MY EYES.
MY AMARANTH AND SWEET PERFECTION,
WHICH MANY SAY NEVER DIES.
YOU HAVE BEEN MY SHINING LIGHT,
WHEN I LOST MY SO-CALLED FRIENDS.
AND IT WAS YOU WHO LIFTED ME UP,
DESPITE ME FAILING AGAIN AND AGAIN.
YOU HAVE BEEN MY LIGHT IN DARKNESS,
I MEAN MY MIDNIGHT STAR.
WHO HAS HELPED ME TO STAY STRONG,
WHEN OTHERS WERE FALLING APART.
YOU HAVE BEEN MY PARADIGM OF LOVE,
THOUGH ALL MY RIGOROUS STRUGGLES.
THE ESSENCE OF A REAL WOMAN,
WHO STAYED DOWN FOR A BROTHER.

77.

MADEMOISELLE

IN THE WAKE OF INNOCENCE,
YOUR LIPS BEAUTIFULLY UNFOLD.
ENTICING MY VERY NATURE,
AND THE REALITY IT COMPOSES.
THE CURLY LOCKS OF YOUR HAIR,
AND THE GLEAM IN YOUR EYES.
PROPELS THE MIND TO GRAVITATE,
TOWARD A NATURAL HIGH.
THE SILKINESS OF YOUR GOWN,
WHICH DELINEATES YOUR WAIST.
INTRIGUES ME BEYOND WORDS,
LIKE THE BEAUTY OF YOU FACE.
IN WAKE OF INNOCENCE,
MY LOVE IS PASSIONATE RENEW.
BY THE TENDERNESS OF YOUR TOUCH,
AND BEAUTY WITHIN.

78.
WISHFUL THINKING

SEIZE THE MOMENT WITH A KISS,
FOR TONIGHT WILL BREATHE OUR LOVE.

NOTHING CAN IMPEDE SUCH FEELING,
WHICH DESCEND FROM ABOVE.

LAUGHTER WILL BE OUR REMEDY,
TO MOLLIFY OUR FEARS AND PAINS.

STRENGTH WILL BE OUR HOPE,
AS WE EMBRACE THE LIGHT OF CHANGE.

STILL, I PONDER ENDLESSLY,
FOR TOMORROW IS DIVINE.

LEAVING TODAY FOR A BETTER AMUSEMENT,
AS WE JOURNEY THROUGH TIME.

79.
IMAGES OF YOU

LOOK DIRECTLY INTO THE MIRROR,
WITHIN THE REFLECTION YOU'LL SEE MY EYES.
FOR IT'S THE WINDOW TO MY SOUL,
AND THE THINGS I ANALYZE.
SOME SAY THE MIRROR SPEAKS SOFTLY,
TO THE MOST PERCEPTIVE HEART.
YOU CAN FEEL IT'S INSPIRATION,
LIKE FROM YOUR MOST INTIMATE THOUGHTS.
THE NATURAL MYSTIC OF ITS BEAUTY,
AND THE UNIQUENESS OF ITS DESIGN.
WILL ELEVATE YOU HIGHER AND HIGHER.
BEYOND THESE EARTHLY SKIES.
WITH THESE THOUGHTS OF EUPHORIA,
I CLOSE MY EYES AND ROAM.
WHILE FEELING THE POWER OF LOVE,
GRACEFULLY TAKING FORM.
REFLECTION OF ME, MYSELF AND I.,
CONTINUE TO EMERGE THROUGH THE LIGHT.
FINDING THE TRUTH OF WHO I AM,
THAT WAS ONCE HIDDEN FROM MY SIGHT.

80.

ISIS

You are my rising sun,
You are my precious star.
You are my conception of love,
Which is forever more.

You are my jasmine flower,
You are my eloquent grace.
You are my picture of happiness,
Each time we embrace.

You are my romantic song,
You are my natural high,
You are my vision of angels,
Who are beautifully disguised.

You are my Nefertiti
You are my Nubian queen.
You are my sweet perfection,
Which many haven't seen.

You are my answered prayer,
You are my guiding light.
You are my pillow of comfort,
On sleepless nights.

You are my quiet storm,
You are my delightful grace.
You are my heavenly blessing,
Which can never be replaced.

81.

NZINGA

MY BLACK QUEEN,
YOU ARE BEAUTIFUL AND UNIQUE.
A GIFT UNTO MANKIND,
WHO APPRECIATES YOU EQUALLY.
PETITE AND ALLURING,
IS YOUR CURVACEOUS FIGURE.
WHICH INTRIGUES ONE'S IMAGINATION,
FAR BETTER THAN ANY PICTURE.
YOU ARE AN ANGEL IN HUMAN FORM,
WHICH MANY HAVEN'T SEEN.
THE CONCEPTION OF REALITY,
THAT SOME MAY CALL A DREAM.
PARADISE ON MOTHER EARTH,
HOW COULD ONE EVER IMAGINE?
WHERE LOVE BECOMES REVEALED,
IN THIS ROMANTIC FASHION.

82.
THAT SMILE OF YOURS

WHEN I STARE DEEPLY INTO YOUR LOVELY EYES,
YOU MAKE INCREDIBLE EMOTIONS GO OFF INSIDE.
GENTLY, MY MIND DRIFTS INTO YOUR ENTICING WORLD,
KNOWING YOU ARE BY FAR MY MOST FAVORITE GIRL.
TH SUNSHINE RAYS WILL NEVER BRIGHTEN MY DAYS,
LIKE THE SMILE I SEE THAT COVERS YOU FACE.
YOUR ESSENCE ALONE CAPTIVATES MY INNER SOUL.
AND I PROMISE TO GOD, YOU ARE MORE PRECIOUS THAN GOLD.
BUT IF THERE WAS A JOURNEY OF ONE THOUSAND MILES,
I WOULD WALK EVERY INCH OF IT TO SEE YOUR LOVELY SMILE.

83.

I THINK OF YOU

I THINK OF YOU IN MY ARMS,
AND THE BEAUTIFUL THOUGHTS OF US.
I THINK OF YOU APPEASING OUR STORM,
THAT COULD ONLY STRENGTHEN OUR TRUST.
I THINK OF HOW LONELY I'VE BEEN,
EVER SINCE YOU SAID "GOODBYE".
WONDERING WOULD YOU EVER RETURN?
FROM THE TEARS I'VE CRIED.
WHEN YOU SAID THAT "YOU LOVED ME",
I THINK OF THAT TOO.
KNOWING OUR LOVE WAS SPECIAL,
DESPITE THE THINGS WE WENT THROUGH.
NOW I SIT IN SILENT PRAYER,
THINKING AS I MOSTLY DO,
HOPING THAT AN ANGEL OF LOVE,
WOULD DELIVER THIS POEM TO YOU.

84.
CALL TO OUR MOTHER

CALL TO OUR MOTHER,
YES!! CALL HER INDEED.
LET US SHOW OUR APPRECIATION,
FOR THE LOVE WE RECEIVED.
BY CHERISHING HER ESSENCE,
LIKE THE AIR WE BREATHE.
WHO HAS GIVEN US THE HOPE,
TO STRIVE AND SUCCEED.

CALL TO OUR MOTHER,
YES!! IN BOTH TRUTH AND DEEDS.
LET US SHOW OUR APPRECIATION,
FOR THE GOALS SHE'LL ACHIEVE.
BY REVERING HER ACCOMPLISHMENT,
LIKE THE AIR WE BREATHE.
WHO HAS GIVEN US THE WISDOM,
TO FOLLOW HER LEAD.

CALL TO OUR MOTHER,
YES!! EVERY SISTER AND QUEEN.
LET US SHOW OUR APPRECIATION,
FOR THE VIRTUES SHE BELIEVES.
WHO HAS BEEN OUR INSPIRATION,
IN OUR TIMES OF NEED.

CALL TO OUR MOTHER!!

85.

ANTIQUITY

STRONG BLACK AND BEAUTIFUL,
THIS IS WHAT WE ARE IN ONE.
SHINING RADIANTLY,
BENEATH THE CANOPY OF THE SUN.
WHEN UNITY IS COMPOSED,
NOTHING CAN EXTINGUISH OUR FLAME.
WE BLAZE THE NIGHTLY SKIES,
WITHOUT LOSING OUR AIM.
FOR THERE'S NO ABJURATION,
OF A STRONG BLACK NATION.
WHO STANDS FOR FREEDOM AND JUSTICE.
WITHOUT ANY HESITATION.
WE ARISE TO THE OCCASION,
WHENEVER OUR FAITH IS TESTED.
AND WE LEAVE BEHIND INSPIRATION,
FOR OTHERS WHO ARE FALSELY ARRESTED.
LIKE THE AMARANTH FLOWER,
THAT GROWS SO BEAUTIFUL AND STRONG.
SO ARE THE PEOPLE OF ANTIQUITY,
WHO DIED FOR THEIR OWN.

NEPENTHE

Inspirational Quotes

1. "The ends you serve that are selfish will take you no further than yourself. But the ends you serve that are for all in common, will take you into eternity." Marcus Garvey
2. "For the man who has conquered his mind, it is his greatest friend, but for the man who fails to do so, his mind will be his greatest enemy." Sri Krna
3. "I learned that courage was not the absence of fear, but the triumph over it. The brave man is not he who does not feel afraid, but he who conquers that fear." Nelson Mandela
4. "The power which you possess is but one side of the coin; the other side is responsibility. There is no power or authority without responsibility and he who accepts the one, cannot escape or evade the other." Emperor Haile Selassie I
5. "No matter what may befall a human being, he can always succeed in overcoming it if he has the strength of faith and prays to God for inevitably, he comes to the assistance of those who believe in Him and those that, through their work live an exemplary life." Emperor Haile Selassi I
6. "Peace is the diploma you get in the cemetery." Peter Tosh
7. "I can be changed by what happens to me, but I refuse to be reduced by it." Maya Angelou
8. "I have always believed that you help people one at a time. That's how lives are changed." Oprah Winfrey
9. "I'm finally ready to own my own power, to say 'This is who I am.' If you like it, you like it and if you don't, you don't so watch out. I'm gonna fly." Oprah Winfrey

10. "It is now long ago that I … resolved that I would permit no man no matter what his colour might be, to narrow and degrade my soul by making me hate him." Booker T. Washington

11. "Hatred toward any human being cannot exist in the same heart as love to God." William Ralph Inge

12. "God provided me with the strength I needed at the precise time when conditions were ripe for change. I am thankful to Him every day that He gave me the strength not to move." Rosa Parks

13. "I find that if I am thinking too much of my own problems and the fact that at times things are not just like I want them to be, I do not make any progress at all. But if I look around and see what I can do, and I do it, I move on." Rosa Parks

14. "A man of genius is unbearable, unless he possesses at least two things besides: gratitude and purity." Friedrich Nietzsche

15. "To defend one's self against fear is simply to insure that one will, one day be conquered by it, fears must be faced." James Baldwin

16. "The belief that God will do everything for man is as untenable as the belief that man can do everything for himself. It too, is based on a lack of faith. We must learn that to expect God to do everything while we do nothing is not faith but superstition." Martin Luther King Jr.

17. "Hatred and bitterness can never cure the disease of fear; only love can do that. Hatred paralyzes life; love releases it. Hatred confuses life; love harmonizes it. Hatred darkens life; love illumines it." Martin Luther King Jr.

18. "Our lives begin to end the day we become silent about things that matter." Martin Luther King Jr.

19. "To comprehend with your heart what your mind cannot fathom is the beginning of understanding." Perry A. White

20. "Chains of habit are too light to be felt, until they are too heavy to be broken." Warren Buffet

21. "If we have the capacity to endure, if we have the patience, things will change." Cesar Chavez

22. "We ask ourselves, who am I to be brilliant, gorgeous, talented and fabulous? Actually, who are you not to be? You are a child of God. Your playing small doesn't help the world. There's nothing enlightening about shrinking down so someone won't feel insecure around you. We were born to make man into the glory of God that is within us. It's not just in some of us, it's in everyone." Nelson Mandela

23. "The day that hunger is eradicated from the earth there will be the greatest spiritual explosion the world has ever known. Humanity cannot imagine the joy that will burst into the world on the day of that great revolution." Fredrico Lorca

24. "Everything that irritates us about others can lead us to an understanding of ourselves." Carl Jung

25. "None of us has the power to make someone else love us, but we all have the power to give away love, to love other people. And if we do so, we change the kind of person we are, and we change the kind of world we live in." Rabbi Harold Kusher

26. "There are no secrets to success; don't waste time looking for them. Success is the result of perfection, hard work, learning from failure, loyalty to those for whom you work, and persistence." Colin Powell

27. "Learning without wisdom is a load of books on a donkey's back." Zora Neale Hurston

28. "You can't depend on your judgment when your imagination is out of focus." Mark Twain

29. "The reason we cannot see truth is not that we have read enough books or do not have enough academic degrees but that we do not have enough courage." Rollo May

30. "Don't judge each day by the harvest you reap, but by the seeds you plant." Robert Louis Stevenson

ABOUT THE AUTHOR

This book, NEPENTHE, A Taste of Inspiration, is the author's first book in print. A cursory review of the poetic contents clearly reflects the universal vicissitudes of the African-American, the Caribbean, and the African people.
Most of the author's aspirations and Afrocentric thoughts came from the numerous leaders and teachers on the front of the book cover.
In addition to this book, the author has a sequel book coming out called Poetic Jewels of Serenity and Rudeboy Mercenary.

www.ingramcontent.com/pod-product-compliance
Lightning Source LLC
Chambersburg PA
CBHW071858070526
44583CB00016B/1741